PASSION
INSPIRES
GREATNESS

PASSION
INSPIRES
GREATNESS

A JOURNEY WITH PURPOSE

MARALA SCOTT

 Seraph Books

Published by Seraph Books, LLC
www.seraphbooks.com

ISBN Hardcover: 978-1-941711-22-4

ISBN Paperback: 978-1-941711-23-1

ISBN E-Book: 978-1-941711-24-8

Library of Congress Control Number: 2017943618

PRINTED AND BOUND IN THE UNITED STATES OF AMERICA

10 9 8 7 6 5 4 3 2 1

Cover design by Alyssa M. Curry

Copyediting by Alyssa M. Curry

Author photo by Alyssa M. Curry

For information regarding special discounts for bulk purchases of this book for educational, gift purposes, as a charitable donation, or to arrange a speaking event, please visit: www.maralascott.com

www.maralascott.com
Twitter: @MaralaScott
www.facebook.com/maralascott

To the parents, teachers, mentors, coaches, spiritual leaders, and individuals who work passionately to inspire greatness, and to those who work tirelessly to achieve it.

There are times when your passion has to come through with tremendous power so you can go after what you want as if everything is at stake.

– Contents –

CONTENTS

Passion is something you can feel more intensely than anything else. And when you do, it is something that will not go away. If, by chance, you miss your mark, true passion will drive you to learn, grow, and continue in your efforts until you achieve your goal. Passion inspires greatness.

- Introduction -

There are many lessons to come.
Make peace with life. It is not your enemy;
it is your teacher.

~ MARALA SCOTT ~

I believe in inspiring people just as others inspired me along my journey. It is my way of stimulating someone's heart, soul, and mind so they can reach their best potential in many areas of life and take *a journey with purpose.*

You are not in a race to get to the end of life, which is why you have so many lessons in between. Slow down and learn them. Challenges will test and develop your strength and character. New places and people will provide exposure and open your mind to things you must experience, learn, and feel. There are people who will teach you what others could not or what you stubbornly refuse to accept. Some of those lessons may be painful and others beautiful, but you will have them. Life will offer a greater discovery and understanding of yourself, and some of those things will lead you to your passion.

Passion Inspires Greatness will teach you valuable lessons on how to build a strong foundation for life and bolster your confidence. It addresses ways to avoid and overcome adversity. It will help you identify aspects of your character that are helping or hurting your advancement. You will become conscious of the things that could be derailing your progress. As you take in these lessons, determine if what you say you love is *truly* passion.

Passion is something you can feel more deeply than anything else. It drives, pushes, and forces you into an emotional place of need where *you feel inspired to do something about it*. When you create a plan on how to achieve your goals, you've reacted to an inspirational tug that can introduce you to incredible opportunities.

Inspiration can change your life and give you both the vision for what you truly want and the power to create it. One of the greatest advantages of inspiration is that it pulls you toward aspirations rather than pushing or forcing you in its direction. It is magnetic and captivating and will cause you to do something of your own free will. Sometimes, through inspiration, it is merely the opportunity you have created. However, the opportunity is all that is required to renew hope and elevate consciousness in order to bring your desires and ambitions to fruition.

In one form or another, and every minute of

the day, there is an infinite supply of negativity being spread around the globe. Too often, you are reminded of what you cannot do rather than what you can. You are fed doubt, deprived of confidence, ridden with pessimism, and scarred with disapproval; creating the desperate need for inspiration. *And it works.* Inspiration feeds you positive affirmations that deliver creativity, produce direction, and fill you with purpose. It is the transfer of positive energy and it is my way of giving people ammunition to combat negativity so they can move into a healthier state, where they belong—and where *you* belong.

Throughout each day, billions of people utilize something that is powerful and uplifting if used in a positive manner. That same thing can be a weapon of destruction to the mind if used with negative intent. You can read, write, and speak them any way you choose, as they are *words*. Words are powerful and assembled to express love, compassion, understanding, discord, knowledge, direction, healing, and inspiration. They can shape your thoughts, as well as change, encourage, and take lives. That is why it's imperative to fill your mind with the best combination of them. What we feed our mind is what we believe we are. What we visualize is what we see ourselves accomplishing. The things we allow to touch our soul can lift or suppress it; so consequently, our passion will either live or die.

If you want to accomplish anything *great* in life, allow your passion to inspire you to *consistently* have a strong work ethic to achieve greatness. Don't wait for someone to constantly coerce you to achieve success. Go willingly and you will be more likely to persevere. Be inspired to get up and continue trying even after you fail, because failure is an unrelenting teacher. It will keep testing you until you quit or achieve success.

I cannot say what achieving greatness means to each individual as we all have distinct goals. For some, it is to survive extraordinary or life-threatening circumstances; while for others, it may be to save lives from those same circumstances. Achieving greatness may include being considered among the greatest athletes, entertainers, entrepreneurs, and so on. It may be to do what others say you cannot, create something beneficial to mankind, or to simply *inspire others*. Whatever that is, only you know—and you already have the passion inside of you. It is in each of us. Yet, it is adversity, lack of confidence or faith, fear, distractions, a negative attitude, or poor work ethic that can keep you from not only feeling, but also not acting on your passion. Release your passion from that space where it cannot breathe and allow it to manifest and inspire the greatness in you. *My goal is to passionately inspire you to achieve greatness.*

- Note to the Reader -

When you are afraid, you are choosing to let fear in. If it is your goal, dream, or path to success, understand fear cannot exist. Make it happen.

~ MARALA SCOTT ~

*P*assion *Inspires Greatness* was written to challenge you to determine what your passion
is, deliberately seek inspiration, and consistently practice a strong work ethic as it is the
prerequisite of success.

Allow *this book* to help you understand the
things you will encounter along your journey and
provide the tools to overcome adversity, renew passion, create focus, and a clear vision of success.

At the end of each chapter, I have shared my
personal inspirational messages that are powerful
pieces of reality I've written throughout the years.
These are the things I have done to overcome
or avoid adversity. They are the lessons I have
encouraged others to utilize throughout their
journey to help them find their passion, purpose,

and achieve goals. May you feed them to your mind, embed them in your heart, and find value and comfort in them as needed.

When you come to understand the power of inspiration, pass along the lessons you've learned and inspire others.

PASSION
INSPIRES
GREATNESS

- 1 -

STABILITY

CREATING A STRONG FOUNDATION

Build a foundation that will last through the most difficult storms so you will be confident when they come.

~ MARALA SCOTT ~

Throughout your childhood, adolescence, and adulthood you were taught a variety of things, among them were the basics of life. You may have dismissively ignored a few, but you *are* familiar with them. You've been educated on having good character and its components, such as integrity, honesty, the difference between right and wrong, and so forth. Even if you don't exercise good leadership skills, you were taught how, and know when you should apply them. The lectures and lessons about respecting others, especially your elders, were continual. You have learned what love, friendship, and loyalty are and you know what they are not. You can make the distinction between good and poor health and you can often feel when something is wrong, as there is a beginning to everything.

You crawled, stood, walked, and then ran. You drank from a bottle, cup, and eventually a glass. You learned to ride a bike, and subsequently, drive a car. You went from kindergarten to first grade and so on.

From the onset, you've learned to set and achieve goals. You've experienced what confidence is and you know what it is not. Then, somewhere, somehow, you've discovered what passion is. But one of the biggest lessons of your childhood may have been about faith. Along the process you have had countless lessons, mastered skills, and hit milestones. It doesn't mean that there was one specific individual who taught you each lesson, but you were taught because, in some capacity, you would need them. Using them at the right time and in the appropriate manner will be key. And when you realize that you've formed a few bad habits, go back to the beginning and determine what went wrong.

Now you are at a point in your life when it is critical to your personal growth and the level of success that you will achieve to use the things you have been taught. This journey you are on, called "life," will demand that you construct your foundation well, because its strength and stability will be tested. Your foundation will help support the individual you work toward becoming and if it doesn't turn out so well, take responsibility, because you are the one building it.

Just like building a house, the footing anchors it to the ground and supports the foundation, which carries the weight of the house. In essence, the foundation has to be able to handle everything that is going to be placed on top of it. The same goes for you. You need to be able to handle what comes at you in life so you are strong enough to learn from it and then overcome adversities without your foundation falling apart. If your foundation is not built well enough, it could be an opportunity lost.

Your footing or anchor should be your *faith* and the foundation should be comprised of *passion, excellent character, confidence, mental toughness,* a *positive attitude, strong work ethic,* and *discipline.* As you build upon those areas, you will add more intricate components; their value is vital to the level of success you will achieve. *Remove one, and you will weaken the foundation.*

As you continue learning and gaining experiences, you are developing as an individual. The goal is to be certain that anything you place on top of your foundation is good for you. Why? In essence, you are constructing who you desire to be. This is a good time to ask yourself if you love what you are building.

Loyalty is something to consider, as it is significant in your personal life, business, and athletics. If you want to be a great leader and inspire loyalty in others, be honest, authentic, supportive, fair, and willing to mentor or share ideas to help others develop. If you are loyal to no one, your contribution and value to others is diminished. And if you are part of a team, that displays your inability to work with the team for the overall goal.

If you care to look at the bigger picture as far as loyalty is concerned, ask yourself a few questions. Are you loyal to others? Are you loyal to your routine or the program? Are your coaches and teammates loyal to you? Do they exhibit trust and confidence in you? You should know the answers, but if you don't, it's depicted in their communication and interaction with you, so pay attention.

Everything you do on and off the field, court, or at work, affects your team as a whole. If you make a poor decision, it could cost them an opportunity to succeed or win. If you are not loyal to your workout routine or disciplined in other behaviors, it could hurt them too. A team needs everyone on it to be well-prepared every time they compete. Why? Loyalty to oneself is detrimental to the process. Again, the question is, do you believe yourself to be a loyal person?

Loyalty is what great athletes are made of. If you want to learn how to be loyal, identify your purpose, let go of the small things, model the behavior that you expect of others, and make loyalty a part of your character so it becomes a part of your lifestyle.

Self-control is necessary to overcome undesirable behaviors that may be addictive, obsessive, or destructive. The point is to exercise self-control at all times; be especially conscious of it when you are trying to achieve a goal.

Control is something that can be lost at any given moment for a multitude of reasons so no one really owns it. It is when you are tempted to act, perhaps on impulse or in the moment, that you will lose control. This is why it is important to learn and apply techniques to help you manage it. Self-control is a way of making the choice to manage your dominant behaviors. But at times, you may have used up your ability to do so and become depleted, making it more difficult or unmanageable. That's when you need to pull back, evaluate your behavior before it reaches the point of no return, and determine what is causing you to let go.

Find a way to exercise self-control so you can take charge of your life by having healthy outlets to release stress and anxiety. When you lose control, you are giving the *illusion* of control to others, and you may not like the person or people you are giving it to. Consider the social environment that you engage in or your personal environment and determine if you need to make changes. Is there something that facilitates stress or produces inflammatory behavior? Do you have unresolved personal issues from your childhood that cause you to lose control when they are triggered? Whatever it is, do not let it build up and damage your health. And take under consideration that when you lose control, you have the ability to negatively affect others.

There are people that will identify your lack of self-control as a weakness and use it to their advantage in competition or when it is critical to exposing your character. Being great does not mean you are great when things are going well. What it means is that you apply self-control when they are not. By now, you know yourself and what causes you to lose it. When you find yourself in a situation that threatens to disrupt your state of mind, step back and then consider the bigger picture and the consequences. Think about the outcome, what it will do to you and how it will affect others. Work to apply self-control in moments that try to draw you away from it. It is a test of your mental toughness, confidence, and willpower. Pass the test!

Excellent health is something you must consistently work to maintain. When you are building a foundation, being strong and healthy is a key component. Your success is not solely predicated upon maintaining good mental health; your physical health has a great deal to do with it. When you are healthy, you are more confident in your abilities. Consistently eating healthy, exercising, and getting enough sleep is just the beginning. Reduce stress and do the things that make you happy but be cognizant that *you* are in charge of your happiness, no one else. Don't be afraid to enjoy your journey and pause to make sure you are protecting your health. When you do that, you are investing in your future.

It's not too late to invest in stabilizing your foundation. Remove the things that can weaken it or become problematic and don't forget to add the necessary reinforcements. There is strength in numbers and the number of positive attributes you add to your foundation will help you succeed in life.

Have you invested in building a strong foundation? If so, how?

INSPIRATIONAL GUIDANCE

+ Be careful what you say when you are emotional. Once you verbalize your thoughts and put those feelings out there, others' feelings towards you may change.

+ Stay focused on your progress and personal development. Do the work and don't lie to yourself or you will lie to others too.

+ Having self-control, being disciplined, and achieving greatness requires sacrifices. Do not engage in negativity—stay focused. Less now can bring more later.

INSPIRATIONAL GUIDANCE

+ Keeping company with negative people will shape your thoughts and impede your progress. Break the cycle and change your course.

+ Sometimes, temporarily withdrawing from people will show you those who are drawn to you for the right reasons. Genuine love and loyalty won't fade.

+ Each of us has something special about us but some have yet to discover what that is. Part of your journey is discovering who you are.

INSPIRATIONAL GUIDANCE

+ Life is a journey. It is your journey, but there are parts of it that will require you to move, think, and react as part of a team in order to succeed, not as an individual.

+ Like the ocean, everything including you has power, depth, and beauty. It is simply a matter of seeing and using it.

+ Being too quick to react can cause you to overlook the situation as a whole. Take your time and trust your intuition.

INSPIRATIONAL GUIDANCE

+ The most difficult task will challenge your mindset so push yourself into the right frame of mind and conquer it.

+ Attitude is a major factor in your success. It influences the way you listen, respond, your work ethic, level of respect, appreciation, and dedication to your faith.

+ Be conscious of the thoughts you manifest, the words you speak, and your actions as they determine your future.

– 2 –

PASSION

DOES NOT EQUAL WORK ETHIC

*There are times when it is not your passion
but your lack of work ethic that keeps
you from your intended success.*

~ MARALA SCOTT ~

I f you pay attention to the way some people communicate when they emit passion, it is absolutely
mesmeric because you can feel it hit your core.
Those who understand the enormity of passion
know how to use it wisely. They are the individuals who accomplish something so exceptional they
want to teach others how to connect with their passion and use it to inspire greatness.

When they work on whatever they are passionate about, it intensifies. Focusing is instinctive and
it is normal for them to willingly invest more effort
than what is required and it can be done in the
same timeframe as their peers. They accept and will
do what it takes to bring their goal to fruition and
understand complacency can be the destruction
of goals, which ultimately suppresses passion. It is

a gift to have passion and gratifying when it is utilized to bring about a remarkable outcome. When passion is authentic, it surfaces organically and it is infinite.

It is easy to express having passion for something but determine whether or not you love it enough to *consistently* sustain a healthy work ethic to achieve your goals. That will tell you if it's real or not. Having passion doesn't mean it automatically translates to having the necessary work ethic to be successful. And it is possible to have one without the other. The definition of *passion* and *work ethic* are often cleverly combined but they are not the same.

Passion is a strong inclination toward a self-defining activity that people like or even love, find important, and invest time and energy on a regular basis. *Work ethic* is a belief in work as a moral good. Although they are not the same, trying to accomplish something or competing without using them together is a mistake as passion and work ethic support each other.

What some people fail to understand is the reason they are unable to accomplish the things they are most passionate about or how to achieve *greatness*. It occurs in sports all the time. Athletes get to a point where they become comfortable and then, whether they realize it or not, plateau. Authentic passion and a solid work ethic do not allow that to happen. It is not something you can easily control and it rarely sleeps. Together, they will keep you working and preparing for the journey long after others have given up.

Consider passion as fuel that is to be used rather than stored. Release it and see where it takes you. It may introduce you to your purpose while exposing the foundation of who you are as an individual. It is priceless. Through the most challenging of times, it can become the driving factor or inspiration that keeps you from quitting. If, by chance, you miss your mark, true passion will inspire you to learn, grow, and continue in your efforts until you achieve your goals. *Passion inspires greatness.*

Take a moment to reflect on situations when your passion has been incredibly profound. It may have been good or even bad, yet there is something that you have displayed passion for. It made you work harder, fight to remove barriers, make sacrifices, or find another path to your goal. Whatever it was, it tapped into your passion and revealed how badly you wanted to accomplish it—except passion alone didn't lead you to your goal.

Due to its depth and ability to be quite deceptive and dangerous, there is more to passion than what some may care to consider. It can be *obsessive* and cause tremendous conflict or *harmonious* and work with you to provide balance. It has the ability to make you think that you are doing everything you can to achieve your goal when in reality you may not be. The emotional excitement can be a distraction where you spend more time talking about how much you love something rather than investing in your goal. Although passion is incredible if it is the right kind of passion, be forewarned that it can be incredibly dangerous too.

We have all heard a coach, athlete, or someone with an unbridled passion encourage or instill confidence in us by sharing part of their journey. The energy around them is positively electrifying. The sincerity inside of their captivatingly fervent words derives from the journey they took to reach that self-defining point. For them, it is not possible to conceal genuine passion, nor do they want to. When their passion hits you just right, the emotional charge will ignite something dormant inside of you that has been waiting to be activated. Typically, those individuals have garnered great success in the area they are passionate about or they have helped others gain success. And if you listened carefully, you heard something greater behind the immense pride. Perhaps it's the sacrifices they've made to get there, the struggles they overcame, or the ability to help others reach their next level or goals. Either way, there is a passion for the game, sport or whatever it is, combined with an unrelenting work ethic.

Keep in mind, you can detect something different expressed by those who have passion but haven't done the work. Their lack of success or inability to reach their goals is the measure. That is the difference between having passion and passion with work ethic that inspires greatness.

Passion is measurable. If you want to know how

far your passion has taken you, look at the metrics. Pay attention to your starting point, measure your progress, and make an honest evaluation of the projected outcome. You will know if the work ethic is there. Instead of taking shortcuts that hurt you in the long run, be dedicated, result-driven, and put in more than the standard amount of work necessary to be great. *Average work produces average results.* Regardless of what else is going on around you, stay committed to improving your skills. Your passion alone is not enough to help you reach your goals. Passion is driven by desire and desire is reinforced by work ethic. A lack of discipline to do the work is an indication that you aren't fully invested.

In any sport, you will find innumerable athletes who are passionate. They have played since they were young, devotedly studied the game, and love their sport. It's what they know. Throw out a name of a great player and they can enthusiastically recite the player's stats or best games. When it comes to practice, they will show up, as scheduled, and complete the required workout routine. But is it enough to simply do what is mandatory? Does their level of effort exceed what is expected? Are they working harder than most or grinding longer than what's required? Do they complain all the way through the workout or can you see passion and determination resonating in their eyes? *Doing what's mandatory is doing the basics.* That is *not* passion and it is *not* work ethic. Being dedicated, dependable, driven, and determined are some of the characteristics of a person with excellent work ethic. *Be that person!*

Although passion for the game may not diminish, in time, the opportunity to play at the next level will. It doesn't take much to discover that what may have worked before is no longer enough. There is always someone on your heels working harder or someone in front of you more relentless. In some respects, the advantage of having a solid work ethic can extend your time for doing what you love.

Many athletes have the desire to play a sport on the next level, but are they willing to do the work that is necessary to stay ahead of the competition? Not the work they think is enough, the work that it takes to go beyond being complacent to achieving greatness. For many, it can become frustrating to want something more than anything, only to find it difficult to achieve; nevertheless, an honest reflection can help. Ask yourself: Have I done everything I can to reach my goal? Do I have the grit to get it done? Do I grind day-after-day and make sacrifices to keep grinding? Do I believe in myself? If not, that's when you need to determine why you have that passion and what the origin or initial factor was that created it.

While your work ethic may be solid, a lack of passion can keep you from progressing. Passion is necessary because it will inspire you to find a way to work around obstacles and push through barriers more than you normally would. If you have the ability to combine passion and work ethic, together they can be comparatively powerful and prove beneficial to achieving your preferred outcome. Rather than ignore or fight your passion, strive to be in harmony with it. Passion plus work ethic leads to greatness.

Initially, you have the passion but will you have it in six months?

INSPIRATIONAL GUIDANCE

+ Understand the difference between harmonious passion and obsessive passion. The latter, obsessive passion, may seem to work initially, but it is harmonious passion that will outlast it without doing damage to other areas of your life.

+ You may not like having to do the work, but knowing it is necessary creates the decision as to whether or not you want to achieve the goal.

+ Don't wish, regret, or be envious of those who did the work or do what you dream of. Fill your life with joy and adventure. Use your passion to become who you are meant to be, which includes doing the work.

INSPIRATIONAL GUIDANCE

+ There are individuals who are visible with their hard work, while others work hard in private. It doesn't matter how you do it if you are really putting in the necessary work.

+ Passion in business, sports, or any area of life can be a driving factor to success, but make sure it has mature emotional behavior.

+ Some people dream and wish it could happen. Passionate individuals create the dream, make it happen, and live their destiny.

– 3 –

CHARACTER

QUALITIES DISTINCTIVE TO YOU

*Do not use your circumstances as an
excuse; use it as motivation to improve
who you are or you will teach
yourself to become a victim.*

- MARALA SCOTT -

.

Observing people in the right setting can tell you a lot more than what they may verbalize. Besides, it's fun to watch others. And you can be assured that they observe you too. There are things about you that tell people who you *really* are. Those particulars leave imprints leading to a key that unlocks the door to *the truth*. The details aren't necessarily about your personality; they expose your character.

Qualities that are distinctive to you is something your journey will reveal. Regardless of how big or small, there will be tests that you will pass or fail, which contribute to either damaging or developing your character. These tests may come from those closest to you, complete strangers, or various situations. Passing or failing once doesn't imply that you have great or poor character; it simply means you have passed or failed. For example, if you give someone a dollar on the street, it doesn't denote great character. It could simply mean that at that moment, you displayed compassion. What matters is when you encounter character tests on numerous occasions and are consistent in passing. That is when you know what your character is.

When someone says, "you have good character" that typically implies an affirmation of your moral qualities. It means that you are the type of person who will determine what is right or wrong when the decision isn't clear. Your behavior is good when people are watching and when they aren't. You care about how you are progressing and the type of person you are becoming.

Everything you do and the choices you make contribute to the evolution of your character. It is beneficial to your passion and the pursuit of greatness. How? People who possess a strong work ethic tend to have strong character. Character creates something that will be attached to you as long as you live and your reputation is largely based on it. Although it's always present, your character is usually something that is brought out in specific situations. Someone may garner judgment by observing your actions during adverse situations, when an ethical choice ensues, or by simply listening to your contradictory, inaccurate, or unethical communication. Some of your past behaviors, which shape your reputation, have the ability to become predictors of your future behavior. The problem with that is they will follow you until you work to change them.

Even if your personality is captivating or charming, that is not a representation of your character. And you know what your true character is. It is you—*the real you*—the one you see in the mirror in the morning and the same reflection that is cast at the end of the day. Are you respectful, responsible, honest, kind, compassionate, and moral? Are you unfair, lazy, judgmental, or racially prejudiced? Those are some of the basic questions to help you take a closer look. Now, delve a bit deeper and ask yourself if you are driven and committed? Do you have personal accountability? Are you coachable or does your ego prevent you from being coached? Do you listen—*well*? Do you harbor resentment or jealousy? Is money your motivator or is it passion? And how do you respond when adversity surrounds you? While it may take time for others to see who you really are, you already know what you are comprised of and *that* is your character.

The factors that helped shape your character are not always taken under consideration because people may not know what they were. Not everyone is privy to the circumstances by which you were raised. Sometimes those traits are modeled after parents, peers, and even taken from your environment. However, by now, you've reached the age where you know better because right and wrong are not a unified concept. Given that your morals and values are a significant aspect of your character, when you realize that you have flaws, *change* rather than accept them. Don't use your circumstances as an excuse. Use it as motivation to improve who you are.

Great character is something that attracts people and it is what excellent leaders are made of. When it comes to being a part of a team, all of the parts have to work together to be successful, meaning people must be able to respect and trust you. Just as teachers are able to identify students with good character, so can a coach. It's revealed in your social network, work ethic, passion, body language, facial expression, eye contact, the way you treat others, and when you have power. Before you take on a role or position that is based on your character, make sure you take the time to assess it. It doesn't take long to determine what your character is when you're honest, and it takes even less time if you aren't. Rather than play the victim, blame others, or make excuses for the way you are, seek professional help or work to develop your faith.

Throughout your journey, your character will continuously be tested, but you can check it daily. Become cognizant of the things you say as well as your behavior and actions toward others. If you fall short, don't accept it; get up and strive to be better. Your network is your choice; *keep company with individuals of great character so they inspire you to learn from them.*

How do you sustain good character when you are in the company of those who lack it?

INSPIRATIONAL GUIDANCE

+ The very things you would like to see in others, be sure to see them in yourself first. Learn from your life lessons.

+ Your thoughts and actions toward others will determine how your life is going. It's a constant reflection of who you truly are.

+ Where you are is not all there is to your journey. You have the capacity to be better for not only yourself but for others.

+ Believe that you are exactly what God created and nothing less: a beautiful soul destined for greatness. Act accordingly when no one is watching.

INSPIRATIONAL GUIDANCE

+ Don't be afraid of making changes, as they will open doors you weren't aware of.

+ Those basic principles that came from childhood are what taught you how to handle the bigger life lessons. When you are tested, pass.

+ Sometimes people believe what they want to believe so they can feel better about their choices. Allow your character to be honest.

+ Determine what you believe in and, more importantly, what you will stand up for or do when no one is looking.

INSPIRATIONAL GUIDANCE

+ The thoughts you manifest will tell you what kind of person you are and whether or not you need to change your path.

+ Some people will do what they have to for their own self-gain, but don't be one of them. Gain with integrity.

+ Compassion is a test of your character and reveals your true spirit. Be willing to make sacrifices without measure.

– 4 –

VISUALIZATION

THE COMPETITIVE ADVANTAGE

*You have the power to design the outcome
you desire through visualization.*

~ MARALA SCOTT ~

A picture isn't worth a thousand words; it's worth so much more but it begins with what you visually create in your mind. The mind is so incredibly powerful that it has the ability to change or shape your life for better or for worse. When you learn how to create successful images through visualization, it can give you a competitive advantage. If you consistently visualize successful images, it can improve your results and performance. Unfortunately, what some people don't realize is that it's the negative picture or something you're doing wrong that tries to resonate with you when you are under pressure. Let's eliminate it.

Visualization is the act or process of interpreting in visual terms or of putting into visible form.

That insight will give you the advantage in mapping out your strategy to accomplish something. It is similar to implementing your strategy in the form of a rehearsal in your mind or watching a movie that you are directing. Since *you* are the director, it will have whatever ending your mind creates.

If you continually envision negative aspects of your performance, it has the ability to impede your progress. For example, comparable to a negativity bias, if you focus on a great performance and an equally negative performance with the same intensity, which one will have more of an effect on your psychological state? Most often, it will be the negative one. You can improve that performance by changing your mental picture, but it takes consistency in your efforts. To be successful, you must visualize yourself performing positive actions with precision; and in time, they will become instinctive. Practicing the technique of visualization can help your performance; it is programming your brain. *What you will accomplish depends on what you see yourself accomplishing.*

One of the best aspects of discovering your passion is when you decide that you are going to do something with it and it becomes a goal. Why are goals important? Whether they are big or small, they are powerful contributors to your success. That is an indication that you are ready to focus and make progress. This is the time to take the next step and create an actionable plan.

You have the goal, now how are you going to achieve it? Great athletes have a disciplined routine because they understand the power in doing small things such as forming habits and repetition. They focus on the fundamentals because mastering them is an essential part of their success, but to get to the next level you have to do more. Make time to practice a key strategy that is crucial for your mental game. It can be a valuable part of the process.

If you want to be successful, visualize yourself completing the actions of a winner and emotionally feel it. Visualization is about seeing yourself complete specific actions skillfully and effectively so when the time comes, you can subconsciously perform the same way you rehearsed it. How will this help? Naturally, as an athlete, you have to possess the physical skills to compete. What some don't take under consideration is that it's crucial to have an even stronger mental game. That is what you are developing through visualization.

If you want to achieve greatness, you have to see yourself being great. How can you expect others to see you that way if you don't? Make it a part of your routine preparation for competition. If you see yourself doing something over and over, your mind becomes familiar with that movement or activity even when you are under pressure. A great deal of your success will be based on your ability to visualize precisely what you want to accomplish. When it's time, you will be able to perform with the confidence you may not have had. The biological connection between the mind and body is imagery. Furthermore, there is a connection between your mind and reality and when you learn to use the technique of visualization, the results can be exceptional. Competitive actions are done subconsciously.

The technique of visualization helps to condition your neural pathways, which is why the actions feel familiar when you perform them. It's as though you've created a comfortable pattern in your nervous system. When you learn to visualize your success, it can enhance both confidence and motivation while reducing anxiety. Taking time to organize your thoughts will help get your creativity flowing so you can visually determine the path to achieve your goals.

Visualization requires you to be in an environment where you can mentally focus. Find that space where it's quiet, peaceful, and you will not be interrupted. It may be when you are lying in bed at night or when you are somewhere by yourself. Begin by formulating thoughts of how you need to see things. The choice is yours and so is the vision. Be precise. Do the fundamentals and see the correct actions that coincide with a successful outcome. Until it becomes a comfortable, mental routine, do it for ten to fifteen minutes three times each day. Make sure you see it clearly but also feel the emotions that go with the actions. After you have created the outcome, visualize it again and again in your mind until it manifests or comes to fruition. Visualizing how you will get to your goal is vital in regard to knowing what you must do to get there.

If you don't know how to see yourself continually completing successful actions, it is time for you to develop your visualization skills. This is critical to achieving greatness. Train your mind to believe that you can see it, be persistent, and then do it!

Do you have enough confidence to visualize yourself performing successful actions?

INSPIRATIONAL GUIDANCE

+ No one can shut down your vision but you. Whatever it is, it is there for you to see and achieve.

+ Confidence in yourself is more important than others having confidence in you. When it comes time to perform, they can't help you.

+ Practice running through your plays and movements the way you need to perform, visualize the details, and see yourself doing it successfully.

+ If the vision doesn't reach your mind, you won't believe that you can achieve it. It happens when you believe.

INSPIRATIONAL GUIDANCE

+ Although it will take focus and consistent practice, stay positive and you will begin to see yourself being successful in your actions. Accept and believe what you see as your true ability.

+ You do not need anyone to believe in you to pursue something you believe in. Each of us has a unique journey and passions to explore.

+ Believe you can. See it and then do it until you accomplish each goal. It is your vision, so breathe life into it.

INSPIRATIONAL GUIDANCE

✦ When you come across something you want, don't give up, work for it. Failure is the experience needed to drive you.

✦ The past has given you strength to reach your potential and God has given you faith and vision to live beyond what you think it is.

✦ What you accomplish depends on what you see yourself accomplishing.

– 5 –

CONFIDENCE

THE DIFFERENCE IN YOUR PERFORMANCE

*If you are not confident in your goals
or dreams, it will be difficult to reach them.
Trust yourself!*

~ MARALA SCOTT ~

It is not difficult to differentiate between an individual who is confident in his or her own abilities versus someone who is not. You can see it, hear it, and observe it at work. They are individuals who move past adversity, face fear, know their value, and are not afraid to take risks. At times, you may have wished you had what they have.

Confidence is the quality of self-assurance in your own abilities. It will allow you to go into competition without fear or doubt. Without it, you will perform below your potential. You may view challenges as impossible rather than believe you can accomplish them.

Feeling good about yourself is displayed in your posture, dress, performance, eye contact, attitude, and the way you carry yourself. Since knowledge is power, be willing to show curiosity and learn new things; it can help you feel more confident. If your confidence is low, your passion will begin to dissipate and you may lose sight of your goals. However, there are several ways to help build confidence.

Preparation is a key factor. When you are certain you have done the work, and pushed yourself beyond the standard, you will draw on that work ethic when you are in competition or doing the task. You will know what it takes and be prepared to give what is required to achieve it.

Sustaining a positive mindset means you do not allow negativity to penetrate your mind nor do you relive negative moments. Stay focused on what is at stake. Negativity can fracture your confidence because it has the ability to find your weaknesses. The people who don't believe in you are the very people that should inspire you the most. They are your fuel!

Don't try to make everyone happy. Realizing you cannot please everyone will alleviate the constant drawback or lack of confidence when you don't. When you know you have done the best you can, accept it. Take pride in who you are and take pride in the work you've done to get there.

Focus on what you can manage. You can manage yourself, but there are countless things that are out of your control. Don't venture too far into things you can't manage and your confidence won't be leveled when it happens. It is arrogance that allows you to think you have the ability to control everything when you can't.

Know who you are. Know your limits, aptitude, level of commitment, and flaws. Understand your strengths and areas that need development. Most of all, do not compare yourself to others. When you don't measure up, your confidence may be shattered.

Faith is a factor. When you are confident in your spirit and the kind of person you are, it looks and feels better. Your relationship with God can give you confidence during the times you need it most. Those things that happen, such as miracles, are gifts from God. Having a steadfast relationship with God will help you establish a more confident way of life.

Failure is your lesson in growth. When you fail at something, it doesn't make you a failure; it puts you in a position to learn what it takes to be successful. It will help you become more confident in overcoming adversity if you take time to analyze your actions or learn from your decisions.

Confidence is something you develop by learning from your experiences. It comes from using positive affirmations when speaking about yourself, extending yourself beyond your comfort level, and unconditionally believing that you are capable. When you are passionate, inspired, and prepared to accomplish great things, it shows when your confidence is unyielding because there is absolutely no trace of self-doubt. Begin your day by saying, "I am. I can. I will. I believe."

Can you think of a time when your confidence was damaged? How did you restore it?

INSPIRATIONAL GUIDANCE

+ Empower yourself with words that will turn your thoughts into reality.

+ Overcoming an obstacle is a way to build confidence. It will force you to face and conquer the challenge or push through limits that you have set.

+ Connecting with nature can help build confidence.

+ Some things will tempt you to change course where you may no longer thrive, but trust your intuition.

+ Make your dream work before you have to accept whatever works.

INSPIRATIONAL GUIDANCE

+ I am capable; therefore, I can.

+ When others doubt you, let it move you to believe what God has in store for you. It is your journey so be confident in it.

+ At times, it is necessary to rebuild with a stronger foundation, then you will be confident.

+ Your uniqueness is the blueprint that can change your journey. Be extraordinary, fearless, and ready.

– 6 –

TRUST

HAVE FAITH IN THE PROCESS

In everything you do, there are systems and processes in place that are meant to help you. Learn to trust the process so it can work for you.

~ MARALA SCOTT ~

Change is inevitable and evidence of it is your physical growth. Look at your height, weight, and physical appearance; nothing is as it once was. The changes came as a process, one that took time. When it comes to achieving goals, there is a way to meet them but you have to trust the process and commit to the work. Trust is a critical element; it takes time to build and time to see the results. If you don't have faith that it will work, it probably won't.

Trust is essential when it comes to developing a competitive advantage. A lack of trust reveals a lack of confidence in the process and leadership. When you don't trust the process, it can be difficult to adapt and adjust when it's critical to your development. What does it mean to trust the process? *It means be present, have faith in leadership, and trust that you will be committed enough to do the work to make the process effective.* Don't worry about what you cannot control. Focus on what you can contribute. Worry is a big distraction to your goals.

Working out, eating healthy, and being committed to a routine is all a part of a process if you want to lose weight, gain strength, or improve your health. In time, you will see the difference. If you don't trust the process and stay committed it is not likely you will have success. Sometimes the expectation of immediate results or success becomes the focus. Be cognizant that the process can take a long-term commitment, even to the extent that it becomes a part of your lifestyle.

Trust is not something that is automatically given, which is why situations can become stressful. If you aren't willing to make adjustments or consider alternatives, it makes it difficult to receive constructive assessments, coaching, or advice, as it may be perceived as criticism. Learning a new way of putting, throwing, hitting, or running may not agree with what you are familiar with, but trust that the changes will be beneficial in the long run. If you aren't willing to learn new skills or adapt to an innovative or different coaching process, you may not reach the success you are striving for. Your coach may assess your skills and conclude that you are better able to help your team in one position over the one you've primarily played. Are you going to quit or dedicate yourself to learning the new position? You may be pushed to work harder to develop a skill that *you* feel you have already mastered. Are you going to grind harder to reach the next level, which will challenge you, or fight the process? If you didn't need support to make the process work for you, there wouldn't be a need for coaches, consultants, trainers, or anyone in an advisory position. But there is and you need to learn to trust them, as they are a part of the process that is the means to your goals. As far as the process itself, it will consist of a series of actions or steps that you must take to get to the desired end result. Respect the process instead of trying to cheat the process because you will hurt yourself and your team.

One approach that may help you adapt to change is to determine what the expectations are that others have of you. Take the initiative to discuss them with the appropriate individuals and, in time, your level of comfort should return. The environment will become less stressful, and you will have more support meeting your goals while contributing to the overall goals of the team. Trust has the ability to create unity and confidence.

What happens when you have analyzed the situation and made a decision that you do not trust the process? Take the necessary steps to establish why that is and determine what it will take to foster an environment you can trust. Are the risks too substantial? Is your confidence in your personal ability not as great as it need be? Does integrity come into play? Whatever it is, direct and honest communication may help. In order for a team to be at its best, in business or athletics, you need everyone to support the overall goals and trust the process. Don't try to control every aspect of your success alone. Passion creates purpose so don't be afraid to allow others to contribute on your journey to achieve success.

Are you confident enough in your leadership or coaching team to trust the process?

INSPIRATIONAL GUIDANCE

+ A change will come as the next season of your life. Don't be afraid of challenges or overcoming obstacles. They will make you better!

+ When you know the weather is changing, change and adapt so it is not an inconvenience or creates bigger problems. Do the same with life.

+ When you make a commitment, be accountable and be that person people can trust.

+ Along your journey, you will have obstacles but don't let one of them be your ego. Be humble and ready to learn.

INSPIRATIONAL GUIDANCE

+ You have things to do each day to help you during your journey. The decision is yours whether or not you will do them. Trust the process and long-term commitment to your goals.

+ Approach things from another view and you will be amazed at what you see and learn!

+ Know when you need a strong team to help you reach your goals and when the challenge is yours alone.

+ Being resistant to a new way of seeing things may keep you from your intended destiny. Be open to life's lessons!

INSPIRATIONAL GUIDANCE

+ Rather than fighting your way through life, embrace it, learn from it, and invest in it so you can enjoy it!

+ It is beautiful to see people work together for a common goal without ego or envy. That's how progress happens.

+ Sometimes people believe what they want to believe so they can feel better about their choices. Trust the process.

+ Know who your network is comprised of. Encouraging people work to lift others rather than tear them down.

ADVERSITY

OVERCOMING OBSTACLES

Adversity is a part of life that will never end. It is something that will challenge then change us.

~ MARALA SCOTT ~

Life has a great deal to offer and its lessons are abundant. Thus far, you've met and overcome some type of adversity as it comes in many forms. Adversity is a difficult situation or condition, misfortune or tragedy. It doesn't end just because you've faced it once, or even twice. It is an aspect of life that is ever-present and for some, it appears more often than for others. Adversity can cause people to quit, give up, or focus on survival rather than progression. It can build confidence, make you wiser, and challenge you to think creatively too.

The way you handle obstacles depends on the way you view them, but first, identify the barrier. If you don't know what the root of the problem is, how can you address and overcome it? Sometimes the obstacles are external, something in your environment; and others internal, with your personality. Is it a habit that you must work to change? Are you afraid? Embarrassed? Depressed? Are you self-sabotaging your success?

Try to understand what happened to cause the adversity and then why. If you don't identify and accept the problem that exists you can't create a solution. Go back to the beginning. The reality is that to do more than just survive, you must learn how to overcome obstacles, and that takes mental toughness.

Adversity can be painful, devastating, and intentionally everything negative. When you encounter it, if you linger in that space where adversity happened or is occurring for too long, you may find yourself remaining a victim of those circumstances. At some point, they may consume you. This is where it is necessary and vital to your mental state to remove yourself from that place or emotional state. If you find it difficult to overcome, don't ignore it, seek professional help and don't feel bad or embarrassed about it.

It is inevitable to be faced with the loss of a loved one, unhealthy or failing relationships, stressful financial situations, injury, health issues, and much more. When that happens, are you going to lose passion or stop pursuing your goals? No. They are meant to challenge and strengthen you. If not at that moment, one day you will understand your journey.

The way to protect your goals from adversity is to keep them outside of these issues and remain determined to reach them. Adversity pulls you off focus and away from your goals. If the goals were easy, they wouldn't be your desired end result, which you believe could be the beginning of something even more incredible. Commit to challenging yourself to rise above whatever is going on. And when you succeed, you will realize that the goal is truly your passion.

A major contributor to adversity is a negative mindset. It feeds the fear. If you keep company with negative people, they will only work in favor of the adverse situation. Negative people will keep you doubting, wondering, and worrying as well as angry, unhappy, and uninspired. If they have been through a similar situation as you, and have not been able to overcome it, their negativity can become yours. More importantly, if you've had a painful past or negative childhood, let it go. Move on and work to sculpt a better future. Keep company with positive people. Draw from their strength and *feed your mind positive affirmations* on a daily basis.

Contrary to what you may believe, one lesson on adversity is that it isn't meant to break you. Of course, that's what will happen if you allow it. But if you can avoid becoming entangled with every bout you see or hear, it's advised. If you are strong in your faith, rely on it rather than commit to pain, problems, and a lack of progress. Don't give in and allow any form of adversity to get the better of you or suppress your passion and ability to be great. Beat it, learn from it, and become stronger for the next round.

As challenging as it can be, adversity is that lesson or experience that will help you progress, understand your journey, or appreciate life and what you already have. It can build character, make you resilient, and help you become more knowledgeable. Don't let it make you a victim and block your blessings to come.

Countless babies are born in adverse situations and the only way for them to survive is to fight their way through it. *Babies!* They don't know any other way to exist other than to fight and it is instinctive for them. It was instinctive for you too at one point. Why is it that with age, adversity seems to become more devastating and impossible to overcome? Who taught you how to have fear? Who taught you that you couldn't overcome obstacles? If a large oak tree was struck down by lightning, blocking the road leading directly to your house, what would you do? You would find another way home. *Find another way.*

Resilience is a necessary attribute of an athlete or individual that has a desire to keep going, without allowing the deficits that life will hurl at them to cause a setback or break them. Your challenges will reveal the truth about your faith, so take time to reflect on how you were able to overcome adversity in the past and study your life lessons. They are a part of your personal development.

When you are bombarded with issues that are challenging or seem impossible to handle and the resolution isn't clear or in sight, step back and rely on your faith.

Are you facing some form of adversity that you have not sought the help that you need?

INSPIRATIONAL GUIDANCE

+ Take time to pull back and let the things that are not meant for you—pass.

+ Don't stay entangled in adverse situations or fight just to fight. It will change your focus and impede or stop your progress. Sometimes the very thing you oppose is meant for you to embrace, overcome, or learn from so you become wiser.

+ Some of the things you view as obstacles are opportunities.

+ You won't always see it coming, but when things get tough, do the same. Complacency can be your downfall, so find a way to overcome adversity.

INSPIRATIONAL GUIDANCE

+ It may hurt, be the hardest thing you've done, seem impossible, or someone said you won't succeed, but you can. Use positive affirmations every day to stay focused and in a healthy mental state.

+ Activate your faith and begin doing the things you've been thinking about without fear or worry of obstacles. Make it happen.

+ Some things are inevitable. When you see it beginning, don't worry, prepare for it.

INSPIRATIONAL GUIDANCE

+ You may have challenges and some will belong to others. Take care of your physical and mental health and sustain inner peace. Love yourself!

+ Your situation can be different than what others may have been through. Some can't relate at all. They may not understand, but God does.

+ Getting to the root of the problem can keep it from becoming a reoccurring obstacle or a permanent barrier. Know what you are dealing with.

INSPIRATIONAL GUIDANCE

+ When you believe everything should be easy, that's when your challenges are the greatest. Be prepared for life so you can overcome adversity.

+ Small strategic moves can help you accomplish the goal.

- 8 -

SUCCESS

PLACE YOURSELF IN A POSITION TO WIN

*I am exactly what God created me to be
and nothing less: a beautiful soul
destined for greatness.*

~ MARALA SCOTT ~

Most of the time, when you find yourself in a position, either good or bad, you had something to do with placing yourself there. Your contribution to the outcome of situations depends on the choices you make. Either you were invested or you weren't. There isn't an in between. Passion and work ethic are instrumental parts of the process and you know if they were present. Were there many distractions? Did you accomplish your goals? Were you confident in your abilities? Did you win? If you won, you contributed to that win and if you lost, well, you gave the same contribution to the loss.

Of course, it's great to win, but in order for that to happen, you must place yourself in a position to win. How? Start by clearly defining your goals.

What is it you are trying to accomplish? Have you determined the timeframe? Are your obstacles internal or external? Are your goals realistic? If you don't know, then you are just going through the motions, hoping something good will come of it. That is not a winning behavior; it is a losing mindset.

Faith is stronger than hope and confidence is better than uncertainty. It is imperative to know who you are and what you are capable of. When it's time to act, do so with complete confidence. The preparation for that moment was done long in advance, over and over again.

Initially, you may not be able to accomplish what you want, but after adapting the consistent behaviors of a winner, you've taken the necessary steps to make it possible. When you know what you want to accomplish, then you can create a precise plan to get there. No plan, no path, no success.

In business, a significant aspect of the strategic planning process is utilizing a SWOT analysis and making it actionable. The same applies to winners; they have identified what their *strengths*, *weaknesses*, *opportunities*, and *threats* are. That allows them to use their strengths to their advantage, improve upon weaknesses, seek opportunities to excel, and avoid or remove threats. If you want to place yourself in a position to win, *don't make excuses*. Be optimistic and fight to overcome adversity rather than become a victim of it. Transition to becoming an individual who is passionate, inspired, and focused on success. That attitude is what contributes to achieving goals. Forewarning: winning can become a habit.

When you observe a winner or someone who is successful, they are less likely to engage in negativity, blame others, seek negative attention, or complain even when they are given the opportunity. Winners are high performers and they live to do just that: perform at an elite level, which is an arena you can't take negative characteristics into and consistently excel. You have to believe in yourself with every fiber of your being, and then do the work to prove it—to yourself.

When others are hanging out, having fun, or wasting time on things that are not beneficial to the process, winners are making their priorities work to their advantage. They sustain focus, eat healthy, and get eight hours of rest when possible. They monitor their success and spend their time around those who are successful because there is nothing average about a winner. It is a mindset and lifestyle, a goal, and then an accomplishment.

As previously addressed, you have to trust the process if you want to succeed, and winners do. They don't try to do everything on their own. They will do the work with an intense work ethic. Winners are willing to take the expertise of coaches or those who have achieved success or possess a skill set and knowledge that is needed. Why? It is a part of the process in which they trust will give them an advantage over the competition.

Success is not easy; however, someone with a winning attitude welcomes the challenge to achieve it. They are willing to do what is vital to attain their goal.

The habits of winners are distinctive and easily identifiable because they do the things that losers do not want to do. *They are driven by results, passionate about learning, have an aversion to negativity,* and *appreciate the motivational and inspirational aspects of life.* They will *fight to overcome adversity* when others may succumb to it and have a *high degree of discipline* evident in their results. They are not threatened by training with others, as it helps them prosper. They can masterfully *visualize their success* when others only hope to succeed.

If you want to place yourself in a position to win, understand that it is a mindset, lifestyle, and passion backed up by an unparalleled work ethic that the average person would not undertake. Surround yourself with positive people that respect your vision. Progress without fear or doubt, as they do not live inside of winners.

If you consider where you are now, are you putting yourself in a position to win or are you hoping things work out?

INSPIRATIONAL GUIDANCE

✦ Do not allow anyone to make you believe you are weak so they can be empowered over you. Be strong and confident in your abilities!

✦ Don't allow anyone to place a label on you. If you do you may just believe it and jeopardize your passion, goals, and future.

✦ One of the best things you can do in life is be present. Don't let the best moments escape your attention. They may never come again.

✦ Dive in and do not fear the work. Preparation will bring you peace when you are in a situation that works to disrupt it.

INSPIRATIONAL GUIDANCE

+ Inspirational words are mentally stimulating and speak volumes to the encouragement of positive thoughts and actions, so let them in!

+ Being alone in silence can bring a deeper thought process with greater considerations and balance to your emotional state. Embrace it.

+ Be aware of the vision you have for your day and yourself. What you see is how you will shape it. Keep negative images away from your focus.

– 9 –

SERVING OTHERS

TIME TO GIVE OF YOURSELF

Consider what you do throughout your lifetime to benefit others, as that is part of your purpose, to serve.

~ MARALA SCOTT ~

Some people are quick to claim they have accomplished everything on their own. It is the self-proclaimed victim saying, "No one helped me. No one gave me anything. No one cared," and that is the furthest thing from the truth. We have all had help, time and time again, but if you don't recognize it, blame your ego. If you do, hold on to your faith because help will come again.

When it's convenient or in those moments of anger or arrogance, one's memory has the ability to be a bit faulty. There has been a parent, relative, coach, mentor, teacher, pastor, stranger, or some positive influence that helped guide you along your journey. In some way, someone provided or was instrumental in the provision of something you needed and *needs* are not always tangible. You may have been encouraged to play a sport, inspired to attend college, or filled with confidence that you didn't have. Because of it, you may be a competitive athlete, college may have prepared you to have better career opportunities, and your confidence places you in leadership positions. There is always someone that has served you well and there are countless others who need the same of you.

Each time someone extends their hand or resources to you, they are displaying the value of being served. The selflessness of others is not meant for you to accept or benefit from and then move on to solely attend to your goals. Repay the contribution by reciprocating any way you feel the need. When people think of serving others, often money and material things come to mind, but there are a myriad of ways to assist. Show compassion, volunteer, or donate things you don't want. There is always something that someone is in need of.

Have you wondered why someone chose to help you out of a situation that didn't concern or benefit them? How often have you been given guidance that helped you stay focused so you could achieve your goals? Has someone taken care of you when you've been sick? How many times have you been inspired by something you've read? Small things are often left without gratitude but you've been served. When you give of yourself it brings joy, appreciation, and gratitude to *you*.

There is a greater impact that each of us can make by serving others. Sadly, some people fight the realization because they are not willing to give of themselves more than what is necessary. Their preference is to remain on the receiving end although each of us has a responsibility or higher calling.

Think about what coaches do on every level of your journey. They facilitate bringing you closer to your goals by developing you mentally and physically. They analyze your abilities, help create a plan to further your development, and continuously bring the best out of you. Intuitively, they know you have value and made the decision to serve you in a capacity to expose it. They determine how you can best *serve* your team. They are constant students of life who teach others what they have learned. In some way, it helped build confidence. Most often, their investment in you extends beyond the responsibility of their job description as a coach or mentor. Their personal sacrifices tend to go unnoticed, but does it matter? Not if they know they have served you well.

To be great at whatever it is you decide to do will demand more than passion, hard work, and a goal. Being connected to your faith can help you observe more than you may have without it. It can inspire you to serve others more freely when you learn to appreciate the things that are continually done for you.

Serving others isn't something that is conditional, measured, or for personal gain. It's not an obligatory or forced behavior. It is giving—of yourself. Give of yourself because it's the right thing to do. The spiritual maturity is more significant than you know. Live with the spirit of gratitude and return it *in some way* each day.

Do you feel others can benefit from you serving them?

INSPIRATIONAL GUIDANCE

+ At times, serving others means you won't try to change or judge them. Encourage them and give them time to embrace it when they are ready.

+ Your passion, creativity, faith, encouragement, love, compassion, and integrity must be authentic to bring value to yourself and others.

+ Give of yourself because you have been blessed with something that someone else needs. It could be as simple as compassion.

+ Understand that your relationship with God is more important than your relationship with anyone else—but it will make you better for others.

INSPIRATIONAL GUIDANCE

+ It's beautiful when you can feel things more deeply than you once did and it brings about a profound sense of gratitude that comes from serving others.

+ We don't know how meaningful our contribution is to others. We can be disconnected as people, yet the connection is greater than we think.

+ There is someone who needs you, more than you need that person, but their gratitude will open your heart even more to helping others in need.

INSPIRATIONAL GUIDANCE

+ Every day we thoughtlessly take something but often forget to return the blessing. Giving is a better way of living.

+ You can see when someone needs help, just look into their eyes. Do not be dismissive to the act of serving others.

+ Reach your goals by making the first goal to strengthen your relationship with God and have complete faith.

+ Leave your mark as having lived with passion because one day this journey will come to its end. Take advantage of now and live in the present.

- 10 -

WORK ETHIC

RESULTS REPRESENT YOUR EFFORT

*You can dream, set goals, and have passion;
however, the necessary ingredient to
make it come to fruition is work ethic.*

~ MARALA SCOTT ~

There are some days when twenty-four hours may not seem adequate enough to accomplish everything you need to get done. Your day may be congested with work, training, commitments, and priorities that make it difficult to set aside time to spend with family or friends. The time you had prior to establishing your goals may not be available because you have work to do. If you want to have an ordinary routine and do just enough work to get by, own the results. Trying to do everything and please everyone is a way to make sure you aren't great at anything. When you are working toward progressing in your endeavors, it is necessary to make sacrifices for the sake of a greater cause: *your success*. Make it a priority to understand your purpose and what it takes to reach your full potential.

Feeling torn or guilty about the time you spend working to become successful may cause you to choose between remaining dedicated and your social life. That's understandable if you are not passionate, fully committed, or confident in your abilities to achieve success. When you make a commitment to a specific schedule or routine, the choice doesn't exist because the solution is straightforward; you keep it. That is how goals are met and passion is sustained.

Dependability is a characteristic of good work ethic. When others have dedicated their time to develop or work with you, or you are part of a team, show up prepared to focus, and *go hard*. Give it everything you have—every single time. Let your results speak volumes for the work you've done. It shouldn't require someone coercing or demanding it from you. It's your goal! Do it of your own accord with passion, persistence, and without resistance. Be someone that others can always count on to show up both physically and mentally.

Occasionally, you may find it necessary to deviate from your work schedule to handle an emergency situation or unavoidable personal matter. It happens. Be sure to communicate appropriately to anyone who needs to be aware of the change in your schedule. Instead of skipping the work and potentially having a delay in your progress, reallocate a time to make it up and grind harder.

Determination to reach your goals while staying committed is another characteristic of work ethic. Understand that as it applies to athletics, when you aren't doing the work, you can be certain your competition is.

Having a goal or specific focus doesn't mean you have to give up everything because you need time to regroup or enjoy life. However, it does mean when you go to work—apply a strong work ethic. Sustain a high degree of *accountability* and ensure that your time is more productive than others would expect. Don't measure what anyone else has done; stay focused on what you need to accomplish to meet *your goals*. Be driven.

When you are *committed* to a goal, you already know what you expect or desire the outcome to be. The only way to achieve that outcome is to remain dedicated to the routine. You have to do the work if you want to win, be promoted, or get to the next level. Whatever it is you want to excel at will take work. The question is whether or not your level of work and commitment is enough. Eventually, time will tell because your results are a clear representation of your effort. If you want to be great, you have to be willing to do what others are not willing to do. There was no way around it for them, and there is no way around it for you.

You may be able to lie to others but you can't lie to yourself. Why would you want to? Reality is patient and it will wait for you because it's always there, even when you refuse to see it. The excuses, delays, and blaming others will come to an end either by you or through the lesson of reality. If you want to accomplish something, even when obstacles ensue, find a way around it or push through it. Obstacles cannot stop authentic passion and an intense work ethic.

Do you believe your results represent your work ethic? Can you do better?

INSPIRATIONAL GUIDANCE

+ Refuse to let others draw you into a negative mindset. It is nothing more than a distraction from your peace and focus.

+ Be determined to make a plan for your life or life will make a plan for you and it may not be the one you want.

+ You know what you need to do but others may not share that goal and your work ethic will set you apart.

+ Be the person you say you are rather than selling who you want to be.

INSPIRATIONAL GUIDANCE

+ When you say you are going to do something, do it with passion and a strong work ethic. The depth of your grind depends on the strength of your mind. Push past the boundaries that were set by others.

+ What you allow inside your mind will dictate the results that come from it.

+ It begins with you. No excuses, distractions, or quitting. Make it happen!

+ Consistency is an attribute that will help you achieve your goals. Make sure to have consistency in faith above all.

INSPIRATIONAL GUIDANCE

+ Pay attention to your surroundings. It will tell you if you must work harder or go create a better opportunity.

+ We wait and rely on others only to find disappointment. We must learn to trust our ability and rely on ourselves.

+ When you go to compete, if you didn't leave it all out there, you didn't take it with you to begin with.

+ You wanted the opportunity and you got it; now do everything you said you could and more. Create a bigger opportunity.

- 11 -

BEGIN AGAIN

RECLAIM YOUR PASSION

Don't quit on your passion or goals;
they need you to exist.

~ MARALA SCOTT ~

You tried, but it didn't work out the way you thought it would. At this point, you are finding it difficult to continue pushing through without seeing the necessary results. You may have thought you were working hard enough, but you didn't make time to do more than what was required. Maybe you did the work but didn't prepare appropriately. And, it's possible that the coaches or superiors just don't see your talents the way others did.

In your previous environment, you may have been a standout, but now things are a bit different. They are putting others in front of you, implying you are not ready. The competition is tougher and you're at the bottom of the ladder on this level. The reality is that you are not proven yet. Mentally, it is difficult for you to accept because you were a superstar until now. Your expectations of your performance were always high and you were used to delivering the projected results. Unfortunately, that was then. Look at where you are now: the next level. It is not the same as where you were and you shouldn't expect the work or results to be the same either. You are going to be challenged to be better than you were before, more knowledgeable, disciplined, prepared, mature, and dedicated. Your execution, focus, technique, courage, confidence, loyalty, and self-control must be elevated. You are in an arena where passion thrives, faith brings confidence, and a strong work ethic yields successful results.

In regard to failure, that's not a bad thing. *Not yet.* Where failure occurs is the place winners are made, greatness is developed, and success comes into view. It is where you get up and begin—again! You can analyze your mistakes, learn from them, prepare better, and move forward. *Failure is your teacher.* It is a fact-checker as to whether or not you did what you were supposed to do. It's critical to have the mental toughness and authentic passion to handle failure because not everyone can recover from its wrath. When you begin again, acknowledge defeat and know what it is so you can let it go. Address it and release it; don't try to suppress that negative thought or it will return.

When you are fighting for something you love and are passionate about, it is difficult to accept failure without bruising your ego. That's what it is. Your ego is bruised because you wanted it and believed you could do it or you wanted to prove something to others. But, you didn't earn it and you didn't win. Don't beat yourself up too much because you need to sustain that passion and a stronger work ethic so you can get there. How do you recover? Take responsibility. The next level isn't for everyone but make it the place where *you* belong.

There is nothing wrong with being disappointed and frustrated with your performance. If you did the work, it means you care, so before giving up on your goals, reclaim your passion. It takes mental toughness to move past negativity, so reclaim that too. Maintain your confidence and get back to work. Take the mistakes into consideration; accept the constructive criticism you were handed; and do it again better, harder, and with more grit. People don't walk into the winner's circle; they fight to get there. Greatness isn't born; it is nurtured. When you make the decision to quit or lose passion, it is because you thought you were automatically deserving of greatness. You didn't think you had anything left to learn but you do, and you always will!

The reason you aren't there yet is because there is more work to be done, lessons to learn, and obstacles to overcome. *You are not consistent!* You must have grit, develop mental toughness, and be determined—all the time. Sustain a need to be successful not only in competition but in life as a whole. Here is where you get up and challenge yourself to transcend without constant setbacks. Stop restraining your passion. Practice more, be coachable, be open to guidance, and listen to *learn*.

The results are your guide. If you are not progressing you are not pushing hard enough. When you don't achieve your goals, consider this: if your workout, preparation, persistence, and attitude are the same, your results *will not* be the same. They will be worse because others who are doing the things you are not willing to do will surpass you. It is time to make changes.

Being disappointed in your results isn't necessarily a bad thing as long as you don't play the victim and blame others. You set the goal. Take responsibility for your outcome. It will only make you stronger, wiser, and more resilient.

Establish what it is that you aren't doing. Perhaps you haven't practiced visualization and have not seen yourself routinely performing successful actions. Are you taking shortcuts? How is your time management? What about your dedication? Do you have a routine? What are your distractions? How is your overall health? Are you accepting of the guidance you have been given?

Be honest in your evaluation because something is missing or not connecting properly. Once you figure it out, make the appropriate adjustments, and get back to work. Grind harder next time. There isn't always a quick fix to something as big as success.

Pay attention to those who are great at what it is you aspire to accomplish because there is a great deal to learn from them. Their statistics don't lie, their passion is real, and their work ethic unparalleled. But they learned how to be successful through the same opponent you will face: failure. While you are pursuing your passion, expect to build an intimate relationship with failure. It will come to know you well, starting with your foundation. Then failure will challenge your character, use your weaknesses and fears against you, and work to remove your faith. Every time it wins, your trust and confidence will diminish. When you grow tired of the relationship, you will either retreat or reclaim your passion and grow wiser and mentally tougher so you can avoid it.

Was there a time when you felt as though you lost your passion? If so, how did you reclaim it?

INSPIRATIONAL GUIDANCE

+ Inspiration can be a reminder of your destiny and keep your goals from dying. They are words that must be put into action.

+ Life will bring storms that challenge your strength but fight it, rebuild, and have faith that the turmoil will end.

+ Courage and fear do not co-exist peacefully for one uses the other as fuel to transcend to new heights, where limitations are not present.

+ When you know where your passions lie, don't leave them dormant, develop your skills to the fullest and be great!

INSPIRATIONAL GUIDANCE

+ At times, the challenge is getting it, but
  the question is whether or not you
  really wanted it. Make a challenge
  meaningful and worthwhile.

+ It is easy to wait and see if your dream
  happens rather than work for it,
  but know there is someone hungry
  enough to do the work and make it
  happen.

+ When someone tries to help you up, be
  appreciative and accept it.

DISTRACTIONS

ANY GIVEN MOMENT

*Distractions can be immediate or subtle but,
either way, they take something away and
that something is your focus.*

~ MARALA SCOTT ~

At any given moment, you can be distracted. It doesn't take much to break your focus but it takes a strong mind to keep it. Distractions are a threat to your ability to focus and will derail your mindset. The derailment may be gradual or it can be immediate, but it will have an effect on your intended goal and the outcome.

When you have something you are passionately trying to accomplish, you should be completely invested. Your focus, commitment, and work ethic must be aligned to maximize their effect. Perhaps you are spending too much time on relationships that impede your progress or invade your time commitment to priorities. Family is typically an Achilles heel because you may feel a need to be involved in anything and everything that goes on—or someone else may think you should be. Regardless of how big or small the issues are, they can keep you from being focused. If the problems grow, personal crises may throw you off course for a long period of time. Those constant distractions can keep you from staying connected to what is supposed to be important to you. If you allow your mindset to shift, how long will it last? Do you tolerate interruptions when you are working on goals? If so, now you know how much of a priority your goals really are.

You may not believe something can distract you enough to affect your performance, but it only takes a brief moment. For example, what can happen if a lineman, whose responsibility is to block for his quarterback, becomes distracted? His quarterback could get sacked because his mind wasn't focused or in the game at that moment.

Have you ever watched a movie and someone entered the room, grabbing your attention? You shifted focus and in that instant, you could have missed a significant point that connected the plot. Perhaps you can rewind, but it is not always that way in life. Those brief distractions can be risky.

Pursuing your passion to be great at something doesn't happen if you are committed some or most of the time. If you want to be *great*, make sacrifices and consistently work to give your goals your *full* attention. That's one of the differences between getting it done and being great at what you've done.

When others do not share your vision or goals,

they can be a distraction in ways you may not want to accept. But when you're off track, even the slightest bit, those who support your goals and want to see you succeed, will notice and address it. Understand that goals are *your* personal ambitions and the passion for it resides inside of you. If everyone were meant to have it, then it would not be as special or significant for you to achieve it. Each of us has unique talents or gifts and our passion can lead us to develop and then use them to the best of our abilities. The only way to know how great you can be is to dedicate yourself and follow through. It is important to realize that having passion means you will have to make sacrifices to achieve your goals. That will include, cutting out things or people that are disruptive to your focus, training, and passion, which takes discipline.

It is to your advantage to identify what causes you to focus. Discover what the best method is for you and be consistent in using it when it's time to train or work on your goals. Use the same process when you are competing or in high-pressure situations. This is life and things happen all the time. If whatever is going on does not pertain to your immediate goal, it is a distraction. Focus and stay there until you successfully complete the task.

When you have something burning inside of you, waiting to get out, it is imperative to the process to lessen distractions and sustain a focused and passionate mindset. As soon as you feel a tug from people or situations threatening to pull you off course, accept the challenge to minimize or alleviate the distractions by increasing your focus. Remember, it is not their goal; it is yours. It is you who needs to respect it and focus, not them. There are times when it is necessary to be selfish and this is one of them.

Do you keep your distractions so you can use them as an excuse when it is convenient?

INSPIRATIONAL GUIDANCE

+ A part of accomplishing your goals and
  having success is being honest about
  where you are now. Distractions can
  slow or impede your progress; know
  if you have any and work to minimize
  them.

+ To be focused and productive, operate
  from a place of peace. Shut out
  negativity and put your goals into
  action. Remove negative thoughts.

+ An aspect of giving away your power
  is giving your attention to the wrong
  things. Distractions detract from your
  focus.

INSPIRATIONAL GUIDANCE

+ Make sure you are well rested and eat properly to avoid becoming fatigued or hungry, which can be distractions.

+ Don't be pulled into a fight that isn't necessary. Anger seeks opportunity and this is a distraction.

+ There will come a time when it is too late. But while you have the time, don't waste it on distractions. Do the work to make it work.

+ When you feel yourself being pulled away, stop it at that moment and refocus.

INSPIRATIONAL GUIDANCE

+ When faced with a challenge, look past it. Give it just enough attention to overcome it and continue your journey.

+ Learn how to manage your emotions, as they too can become a distraction when you are in competition or trying to focus.

+ Stick to your routine or create one that keeps you in the zone. Have a narrow focus.

+ Carrying luggage with pain, hate, anger, mistrust, and doubt is impeding your progress. Let it go so you can live without distractions.

INSPIRATIONAL GUIDANCE

+ A big distraction is when you worry about the expectations that others have of you. That shouldn't be your focus. Determine what you expect of yourself and then do it.

+ Define your purpose and determine what distractions are keeping you from it.

- 13 -

NEGATIVITY

THE DAMAGE IT DOES

*Anger, rage, hate, stress, and substance
abuse are destructive, damaging, and deadly
if you entertain them. The damage they
bring can be irreversible. Let go and live
with passion and purpose rather than pain.*

~ MARALA SCOTT ~

You know what it is like to experience the transfer of negative emotions because it is a part of human nature. You've done it, they've done it, but it has happened. When pressure builds up from stress, it is going to be released in some form or another and when it comes out, often its target has already been identified. Usually the target is the individual that is perceived to be the weakest; the one that shows fear or lack of confidence. Although they may not have done anything to warrant negative behavior, the release was effortless.

The person who carried out the negative behavior may have been a classmate, individual at work, or someone close to you such as a family member. And while it may have been a long time ago, with little prodding, you can still recall what it felt like as well as *the damage or fear it caused*.

Perhaps you are dealing with it presently. Someone is taking his or her aggression out on you by the transference of negative emotions. And if they've targeted you, they were aware they could be effective, which means it probably won't end anytime soon. You've become their release or *someone has become yours*.

Negativity has many methods of revealing itself. Lies, manipulation, physical and emotional abuse, excuses, fear, substance abuse, and bullying are just a few. Part of the problem is that we may or may not realize that stress from our everyday life has the ability to come out or be transferred as abusive behavior if it is not processed or handled properly.

Where does negative behavior come from? Most often, it is learned but the source can go deeper than what you may consider. It can be modeled after someone, and then it becomes a choice to act on that behavior. However, don't make excuses; it can be managed.

If you feel that you are in a situation that can turn volatile, especially at a time you are stressed, remove yourself. If you can't remove negative thoughts or stop harmful behaviors, seek help before it does greater damage. *Do not lay your hands on another human being*.

With all of the professional options for confidential help and support, it is unnecessary to carry negativity. Negativity is a form of adversity. If you can't overcome it, how are you going to attain your goals? Eventually, it will hinder your progress or end it. Before that happens, consider making changes. Talk to your coach, mentor, or a trusted relationship. If you don't feel it is helping, seek professional help and be willing to work through it. Don't view a negative mindset or behaviors as something you are stuck with. It is possible to train your mind to produce positive thoughts that are beneficial rather than destructive thoughts that can do a lifetime of permanent damage.

You may try to convince yourself that what you said or did to someone is over and done with but that's not entirely accurate. It can be forgiven but not necessarily forgotten. Why? Negative behaviors are dangerous. They have the ability to create a lack of trust or fear in others and people have the tendency to remember what they are afraid of.

Negative behaviors can shatter confidence, suppress passion, harm others, or even take a life. People are quick to think they can control their use of drugs and alcohol, but remember, control is nothing more than an illusion that can be taken from you at any given moment. It doesn't take much to destroy your life but it takes faith, confidence, and mental toughness to keep it on the right path.

Substance abuse is a negative behavior that is guaranteed to do considerable damage to the user and anyone who loves that individual. It feeds fear, takes victims, creates desperation, and lies; it can make you do the same. Its grip can sever families, end goals, damage health, cause imprisonment, or even death. You may not want to acknowledge the changes in behavior and lifestyle it causes, but others will, and by the time you do, it may be too late. If you want help, go back to the beginning-- and pay attention to what happened and where things went wrong. The answer is there, waiting for you to work through it and create a realistic solution.

It's easy to give in to injury or adversity with pain pills and other drugs or substances, but it takes a stronger, more confident individual to avoid or overcome it. Transition to the next level without causing injury to oneself or having the delusion of being invincible. Be that competitor who wants to see what hard work and passion will create. Fearlessly and tirelessly grind over and over again until it's rooted so deeply inside of you, you don't know how to stop until you reach your destination without abusing *any* substance. And make sure you *know* your network. Do not allow weak people to make you weak by sharing their pain and problems through substance abuse. They may say, "A little won't hurt," but look at them again, more closely.

It's not productive to become or remain a victim. When there is a problem, acknowledge it at the onset. Things happen, mistakes are made, that's understandable. It's life. But once you recognize or even *think* there could be a potential problem with any form of abuse, seek immediate help to correct it. Do not let your pride get in the way of stopping a serious problem or what could become one. The longer you wait, the greater the risk to yourself and to others. Use pain, frustration, and stress as fuel. Focus on areas you want to excel at and give them your energy in the form of passion.

Are there people who are afraid of you? If so, why?

INSPIRATIONAL GUIDANCE

+ Weakness was not placed in you as God made you in His likeness.

+ Substance abuse is a product of underlying issues. Don't abuse your body and destroy your life because of them.

+ Your fear will keep you from your destiny. Remove it and move past the mindset of impossible and explore life with endless possibilities.

+ Don't let negative people make you negative too. Focus on all of the good rather than getting lost in hate.

INSPIRATIONAL GUIDANCE

+ Although it's been said before, there are times when someone will tell you something you need to hear again. Listen.

+ Do not allow setbacks to keep you from the life you are meant to have.

+ The most difficult task will challenge your mindset, so push yourself into the right frame of mind and conquer it.

+ When you ask for advice, have the discipline and heart to follow through. The advice is free—the work is yours!

INSPIRATIONAL GUIDANCE

+ There are times when you were stronger than you thought possible. In the midst of challenges, remember who you are.

+ I am. I can. I will. I did. I believe. Do not entertain a fearful mindset. Use words that empower and you will achieve your goals.

+ There are many lessons to come. Make peace with life. It is not your enemy; it is your teacher.

- 14 -

RELATIONSHIPS

INSPIRING OR DERAILING YOUR PASSION

*Fear can stop you from becoming
the best version of you. Do not be
afraid of losing relationships that
are not beneficial to your
passion for greatness.*

~ MARALA SCOTT ~

It is beautiful to be in an intimate relationship and have friendships and associations with people to spend time with. Encouragement, comfort, companionship, trust, an emotional connection, and enjoyment can come from them. Sharing ideas or working through personal issues that may surface can be helpful. They may passionately inspire you to pursue your goals because they believe in you. And it's important that you offer the same to them.

The way relationships have the ability to be positive, they have the same propensity to become negative. Negative relationships are toxic and detrimental to the flow of positive progression. They can derail your passion, impede your ability to advance, alter your work ethic, obstruct your focus, *and* stop you from reaching your goals. You may not want to acknowledge it, but that's the reality. People who genuinely care about you and know what you are capable of can sense when your passion and purpose begin to diminish. When true talent in any area fades, it's disheartening. That is an individual who could have made a significant contribution, in some capacity, to the world.

Identify your purpose before opening the door to personal relationships, friendships, and associations that become a part of your network or life. Take time to understand who you are. Discover what you want to achieve, how you plan to get there, and what role they have in your life. Before your joy is suppressed, it is vital to be familiar with the things that make *you* happy and remain connected to them. Stress will take every opportunity to disrupt your life. *Welcome inspirational and positive relationships, but do not admit anyone who will derail your passion for life.*

Relationships can be demanding, which is why it is best to identify and clearly express one another's commitments and personal goals from the onset. If you decide that you want to pursue specific goals during the relationship, have a discussion explaining the vision, plan, and purpose. Transparency and honest communication can help alleviate the feeling of exclusion from participating in your success. How can they participate? Help them understand the demand on your ability to focus so they do not intentionally create conflict. Support from the person you are in a relationship with is essential if you want the relationship to be healthy.

A common mistake is to consider it possible to keep your personal goals and relationship separate. Relationships don't work that way. The negative experiences you have in one area will intertwine with the other and present the ability to affect your performance as well as your relationship. If you care about someone—it is unavoidable but it can be managed.

The best thing to do is create personal relationships that are strong, supportive, healthy, trustworthy, and faith-driven. Your objectives, as an athlete or professional pursuing the next level, are not separate from the relationship itself. You cannot draw a line and believe the two will not intersect, especially if there are children involved.

Healthy and ongoing support is critical when striving to achieve success, which is why it is imperative to address your goals before you find yourself fighting over them. Support comes in many forms but encouragement and minimal stress go a long way. Anyone you've allowed in your personal network should *respect* your commitments and what you aspire to achieve. It is beneficial if they have some degree of passion or enjoyment for what you love. Why? For some athletes, their sport is their identity. The same occurs in business. Be open when discussing the investment of time that is crucial to excel. Don't be naïve to the fact that your focus may limit your availability. It doesn't mean that you will not have personal time to enjoy together, but unless it is scheduled around your work, training, or standard routine, it could produce conflict.

A relationship can happen so fast that time to assess vital aspects may not have been considered. For example, being in a relationship doesn't mean the other individual automatically agrees with the time commitment and sacrifices you must make as an athlete or driven professional. For some, it can be an indication that they accept the benefits of the relationship and are aware of the rules. There is a big difference.

To minimize problems, if you are considering a relationship, make sure the other person understands the boundaries, commitment, and what your pursuit of greatness entails; and make sure to discuss their concerns or goals as well. Be direct and provide honest and clear communication to help alleviate negativity in relationships. Be cognizant that if you chose to be in a relationship while you are pursuing your passion, you are accountable for making it work too.

Contrary to what you may believe, it is not a bad thing to be in a personal relationship with someone who has similar goals or ambitions. And as much as you may be driven to accomplish your goals, adversity may play a role at some point. Injury, illness, and depression are often some of the issues that come into play, and it may require someone who understands and cares about you and your quest for greatness to help you through it.

When it comes to friends and associates, it is good to have them, but you should want to have friends that have goals and passions of their own. If they live for yours, what happens when that comes to an end? If they don't know what it is, help them determine what they are most passionate about and then inspire them. Your personal relationship, family, and friends can be positive or negative. Don't be so eager to surround yourself with people that you overlook the red flags. Establish when it is time to step away. Stay focused on giving your *absolute* best.

Coaches are your mentors, support, and personal team of skilled professionals that were strategically assembled to help you reach your vision. If they are successful, in return, you will contribute to their overall goal for the team. Those relationships should not be taken for granted. Displaying respect for them will aid in facilitating your capacity to understand their vision of what they believe you are capable of. When individuals who possess an expertise *that you need* invest in helping you, it implies they believe in you; believe in them too.

Coaches have many roles. One of those roles is to help you reach your greatest potential. They have the passion to inspire greatness and they know how to get the best out of you both mentally and physically. They can only aid in your development; *you* must do the work to get there. These relationships could be among the most significant you will ever have if it is truly your passion to be great.

Coaches are mentors, advisors, and motivators who will analyze your strengths and areas you need to develop. Their goal is to teach you how to excel, demand more of yourself, and stay focused. They need you to learn everything it takes to perform with complete confidence, which is the reason they help build it. They will push and push to get the most out of your abilities in several areas because they know that is their responsibility. Coaches teach you the game and show you how to progress in your technique by taking one step at a time so you can experience success. To get there, you must establish trust. Using their philosophies to your benefit can help you not only win games but also win in life. Coaches help you sustain balance, focus, passion, confidence, and faith in the process so you have a legitimate opportunity to be successful. If you get out of balance that means something is neglected and in due course it will show. Welcome their ability to teach you how to improve so you can excel. And when your goals are met, their lessons will be instilled in you for the duration of your journey.

Coaches, mentors, or others who have accepted the undertaking to develop you and do everything possible to push greatness out of you should be valued. Those individuals *will not* let you quit without a fight when they see greatness in you.

Analyze your relationships, associates, mentors, and coaches. Pay attention to what you offer one another. Observe those who are working to your benefit and take time to discern the relationships that insert the majority of your stress or attempt to derail your passion and then address it. Do not allow anyone to take you off the path to your destiny. *If you haven't reached your goals and you've been trying for awhile, read this chapter again.*

Are your relationships strong and supportive or are they derailing your passion?

INSPIRATIONAL GUIDANCE

+ If you are not willing to give, don't be so expectant to receive. Life lessons are meant to make you appreciate all of it.

+ Some people will stay in your life for a lifetime, pass through when their season is over, or God will remove them so you can progress. Don't fight it.

+ Don't allow negative people to make you negative too. Focus on all of the good that God has in store for you. Don't get lost in hate.

+ Relationships, friendships, and associations should bring value to one another. That value should be inspiring one another to be their best.

INSPIRATIONAL GUIDANCE

+ Being able to focus is powerful. It has the ability to let you see what is, isn't, or can be. Clear your mind and focus on what is important.

+ Focused means having your mind fixed on something. Handle relationships and distractions without coming off the ladder. Keep climbing.

+ Sometimes the relationships you don't want to sacrifice are the relationships you need to release for your own benefit.

– 15 –

FAITH

CONFIDENCE AT ITS HIGHEST LEVEL

The path to your goals may not appear to be there, but it is. Have faith in your journey, abilities, and the outcome.

~ MARALA SCOTT ~

Throughout your journey, you will come to know or encounter many people, have pivotal experiences, and learn a great deal about yourself and others. Life will tempt you with its vices and test you to see if you can be broken. The challenge is whether or not you will rise or fall. Instinctively, you will make good decisions, but there will be moments when your choices are wrong and now and then, intentionally. Some situations will cause your spirit to be radiant and in others, it may be burdened. You'll laugh from your core, cry when no one is present, and discover things about life that you didn't know were possible. Although you may not acknowledge it, you will experience God's goodness, grace, and mercy. Even with all of the challenges, uncertainty, and unknowns, life is a beautiful journey. It is much more gratifying when it is taken in faith and walked with God. *That is confidence at its highest level.*

Some people can talk to you about anything but find it uncomfortable to talk about their faith. Why? Perhaps they don't understand it or have faith. It could be that they want to avoid judgment or ridicule if their explanation does not match yours. Maybe they need someone to help them better understand what faith is.

Faith isn't for a specific race or religion. It is for all of us. It is defined as a belief with strong conviction; firm belief in something that there may not be tangible proof of. It is the display of complete trust, confidence, reliance, or devotion. Just because you have faith doesn't mean it won't be tested; it will, and it is up to you to pass the test. If you don't, try harder each time until you learn to get it right. *When you have faith, you will know because it is unwavering in the best and worst of times.*

If you try to dissect faith, you can't. Just like you cannot explain miracles. And for the record, every time you board an airplane, skydive, or cross a busy street, you are exhibiting faith that nothing will happen. Remember that lesson about control? You really don't have it, which is why you have faith. Faith will cause you to do whatever it takes regardless of the sacrifice; it pushes beyond reason, it's lasting, and perseveres when tested or faced with opposition. Faith doesn't require proof.

When you aren't focused and connected to faith, it is easy to become distracted by life. If your faith isn't strong, encountering one failure after another can make you lose faith. Why? People need someone or something to blame. There is a need to rationalize or have an excuse as to why you didn't receive what you wanted. The easiest thing to do is to blame someone or something you really didn't believe in anyway, but what does that say about you?

When you make the decision to rise above your own wisdom, you are seeking a life destined for greatness. Having faith doesn't suggest everything will happen the way you want. It means that *you have done all that you can and you will give it to God trusting it will be handled.* Many times it is, but you didn't notice.

You make choices throughout each day and having faith is one of them. When you learn to trust God, you will learn to trust yourself and your intuition will become an invaluable part of your decision-making. When your faith is strong and resolute, your mind and heart will be stronger too. You will be inspired to go to God, above man, for guidance. In time, your gratitude for life will become evident.

Regardless of where you are at any point along your journey, there is nothing that you go through alone because you are never alone. God is always with you. When you make progress and acknowledge the blessings you are given, you will see life differently and approach it from a more humble and appreciative perspective. Success may come, but are you confident that you can sustain it on your own, without faith? More importantly, are you willing to risk it?

For some, the foundation of faith is provided in their upbringing. If it was provided in yours, will you use it to take a journey with purpose? If you want to nurture your faith, surround yourself with believers and deepen your spiritual connection. The same way you take time to learn about other facets of life, take time to go to church and study the Bible. Enrich your life by understanding your relationship with God. Regardless of how busy you get, don't try to fit God into your schedule, schedule your life around your relationship with God. It doesn't mean you won't ever sin or make poor decisions, it means you believe and are working towards living the best way possible. If something isn't working regardless of how hard you try, remember that failure aids in your success *if* you learn from it. What's missing in your life?

Each of us is blessed with gifts, talents, and passion. Whether or not we discover, develop, act on them, and bring them to life is our choice. One of the things that will make a difference in how you view and approach life, is through your spiritual relationship with God. In everything you do, keep God at the center, especially in times of decision. A relationship with God doesn't necessarily mean that life is going to be perfect or void of adversity. It doesn't mean you will always win either, but the relationship will be there with the lessons and experience to help strengthen you. It can help you find peace and contentment in times that are ridden with adversity and uncertainty.

There is much to be said for knowing where the strength comes from that helps you overcome painful or challenging situations. Take time to understand it and rely on it as needed. Draw strength and wisdom from what you have overcome. When everything is going well, acknowledge the blessings. In time, your purpose will become apparent and the path to your destiny, visible. Your confidence will rise to a new level, self-doubt will not exist, and miracles—yes, they will happen.

There are situations that will arise and some may be beyond your ability to manage them, which can create stress, pain, and suffering. Don't believe you must handle them alone. If you don't have faith, it isn't too late. God wants us to come to Him for forgiveness, salvation, grace, mercy, and answers. *Passion inspires greatness, but a relationship with God can inspire you to live the best possible life.* Take time to reflect on the individual God created you to be so you can confidently find and develop the greatness in you.

Do you have faith? Why? If you knew it could give you confidence, would you want to have faith?

INSPIRATIONAL GUIDANCE

+ Worry is a contradiction of faith.

+ When you pray, begin with the truth about your needs; then ask God to give you the strength and ability to help others.

+ Pay attention to where you are headed and you will know if God is guiding your steps.

+ When something isn't working according to your plan, don't assume it won't work. It means it is time to talk to God about a new plan.

INSPIRATIONAL GUIDANCE

+ Each morning when you rise, let your spirit, thought process, joy, compassion, and faith rise with you. Stay elevated.

+ Protect your faith because you will need it. Keep it from becoming diluted with doubt.

+ Align your focus with God by allowing peace to manifest inside of you and don't invite the whispers of negativity or more will come.

+ No one's bigger than a sport. No effort is greater than a team. Have faith and put God above all.

INSPIRATIONAL GUIDANCE

+ If someone comes into your life and you don't know the reason, determine what you asked God for.

+ The next time you pass a mirror, pause and look at how beautifully crafted God made you; with individual goals, unique talents, and gifts.

+ Your faith will be tested and each time you pass you will grow stronger. Believe you can accomplish what others deem impossible.

+ There are things that you must work through. It doesn't mean that no one else cares; the decision and consequences are yours, so ask God.

INSPIRATIONAL GUIDANCE

- ✦ Don't let anyone extinguish your passion, as God was the one to ignite it.

- ✦ Each day is going to bring blessings in some way, but if you are distracted by negativity, you will miss them!

- ✦ Time is not ours; it belongs to God. We put off things until tomorrow but tomorrow is gifted not given. Value today.

- ✦ If you want to feel peace again, release the anger, doubt, and vengeance; then open your heart to faith.

INSPIRATIONAL GUIDANCE

+ We make a conscious decision to hear God and not to when it's convenient. God is your lifeline, so listen closely.

+ The past has given you strength to reach your potential and God has given you reasons to have faith and the ability to achieve even greater things.

- Epilogue -

IT IS YOUR DESTINY

When you feel drawn to something that ignites your soul and it provides a need for you to discover more about your capabilities, grab ahold of it for it is a gift and you are being inspired.

~ MARALA SCOTT ~

You are not meant to aimlessly drift through life. You are on a journey with purpose. It is your destiny to discover precisely what that purpose is so you can activate it and use it to create an incredible, profound life.

Be inspired by life—not afraid of it. Embrace your experiences as if they are teaching you something critically necessary to your development or better yet, success. Adversity is guaranteed, but remember, you are already equipped with everything you need to overcome it. Keep your head up, shoulders back, and faith intact. Do not succumb to negativity, lose passion, or quit. From the moment you were created, you were destined to take a journey with purpose.

You can learn many things but the question is whether or not they changed your behavior.

– About the Author –

Marala Scott is an award-winning author, inspirational speaker, and ghostwriter. She shares riveting narratives that inspire you to draw on life lessons in order to take a journey of healing, purpose, and positive progression, while igniting passion along the way. To achieve goals and excel, she uses the extraordinary revelation found beneath the layers of your life to teach you how to overcome and use adversity as fuel.

Through her prolific inspirational speaking and writing, her efforts caught the attention of Oprah Winfrey, who honored Marala as one of her five

Ambassadors of Hope in 2009 and stated, "A child-hood of abuse almost kept Marala Scott from a life of happiness ... until she discovered how to use her story to help others."

Marala Scott is also the recipient of many awards, among them a Congressional Award for her humanitarian efforts.

Seraph
By
Marala Scott

Seraph is an angel by the highest rank. Seraph by Marala Scott is a line of inspirational cards created to inspire you to be your best, reach the highest level of personal achievement possible, and live as a humanitarian through your expression of passion, faith, and work ethic.

To learn more, visit MaralaScott.com.